T0086280

POETRY
IN THE DARK

MALCOM GORDON

authorHOUSE®

AuthorHouse™
1663 Liberty Drive
Bloomington, IN 47403
www.authorhouse.com
Phone: 1 (800) 839-8640

Published by AuthorHouse 11/09/2016

ISBN: 978-1-5246-4984-5 (sc)
ISBN: 978-1-5246-4983-8 (e)

THE APARTMENTS ON
FIFTH STREET

You want to know what it's like living on Fifth Street? Imagine having a house surrounded by mirrors. Everywhere you looked was exactly the same. Every apartment building was beige, just like the effort they must have put into making them. Plain… Plain… Plain… Income based apartments called the Hamps. Kids would always say, "My mom said I can't go there." Those words echo through the soul of every child who lived in the Hamps. Every child who lived in those Plain… Plain… Plain… Income based apartments. It's funny, really; they surround those apartments in mirrors and expect us not to reflect our environment. They expect us not to reflect those Plain… Plain… Plain… Income based apartments.

"Father Figure"

My mother always told me I needed a "father figure". I never liked that phrase, "father figure". It was like she was blatantly telling me I needed someone to pretend for me. "Father figure," someone to mimic the emotions of father to his son. "Father figure," someone to teach me how to be a man. "Liar," someone who tries to be something they're not. I never found that "father figure" she was talking about. Honestly though, I can't say I've tried looking. I didn't need any more pretenders in my masquerade of a life. I've been surrounded by people with masks trying to hide who they are. Besides, what can a "father figure" teach me? Maybe he could have taught me how to be a man. Maybe he could have taught me that if you lift both parts of the john it's easier to aim. Maybe he could've taught me how to treat a girl. Maybe he could have taught me how to drive. Maybe he could have taught me everything I've learned on my own. Today I found that father. He was looking at me in the mirror this morning. Who would've thought I was named after my "father figure".

THE FAMILY

Memories that stick to your mind
Feelings that corrupt your heart
Parents screaming all the time
It's been this way from the start

Stories told from a different time
A time before I came
A point where everyone was kind
And there was no mention of my name

For some reason it stopped
At the point of my birth
My family fell apart
As if I was cursed

The fighting started
And there was no end
My family departed
No one could win

These are the thoughts
I wish I could forget
They leave mental marks
So mentally I'm sick

This is what sticks to my mind
This is what corrupts my heart
But to this pain I am now blind
And everything I see is dark

So to my family, I'm sorry

STEREOTYPES

Fifth Street was full of stereotypes and racism. From loud Puerto Ricans, to the ghetto black folks and even the dirty white people. We all saw our environment. It was almost like we were segregated unintentionally. The blacks and Ricans never hung out, and if we did it never ended well. As for the whites, they mostly stayed indoors. It was like they didn't want to accept the fact that they were one of us. Normally we all got along; sometimes the Ricans would play ball at the court with us. And when we needed a haircut, they were the people to go to. When it came to the people who lived in the Hamps, we all pretty much got along. I know what you might be thinking, "How can this place be peaceful?" right? Well, for one, just because we live in the hood, doesn't mean we are bad people. Community looks out for their community. Sadly though, we're not the only community. Most of our problems came from the outside world. People coming to our community with unneeded actions and intentions. Although we may have been peaceful to each other most of the time, it's the outsiders that made us react. "For every action there is an equal and opposite reaction," and I must say we definitely reacted the only way we were taught: with violence. See, stereotypes will have you believe that minorities are nothing but a bunch of colored, illegal, unwanted immigrants who only bring violence, drugs, and problems. What a stereotype won't show you is the teacher. Sure, there are lots of black people in gangs, but you must ask, where did they learn it? Sure, lots of blacks are angry and react with violence, but where did they learn it? As I recall, the first "gang" was called a klan. The colors were white as snow and there actions were as dark as their victims. The civil rights movements showed how peaceful protest can get the job done. What it seems to gloss over is the hate and violence and riots that will make Ferguson look like a tea party, just because a group of people wanted to be treated like people. "We did not start this, hate is taught, hate is learned, hate is giving, hate is received." One thing I learned about living on Fifth Street is that stereotypes hide the truth with stats. We are the product of the environment you placed us in. We didn't do it; we just live through it.

LOVE ON FIFTH STREET

I don't know who my first love was. It could be that blondie that broke my heart… but I don't think that was really love. I don't even know what "type" I have. One day it's redheads with two mile long legs, then it's blondes with goofy laughs. But one seemed to burn in my memory, completely different from the default setting of "American beauty". She wasn't tan, she didn't have a big chest or bigger butt, she wasn't dumb and goofy, she wasn't a superstar with ten thousand likes on every picture she's posted since myspace was relevant. Nope, she was pale, thin, smart, pretty, with these big blue beautiful eyes that seemed like they had so much to say. She wasn't anything that the T.V. wanted to sell you. She wasn't fake. She wasn't created from the book called "How To Be Beautiful". Nope, she wasn't any of those plastic expectations. She was something so much more. She was truly beautiful. The type of beauty that can't be mimicked. The type of beauty that no one else can have, because she has the beauty of my first love.

"YOU"

All I want is you
I know that's a lot to want
But I think you're perfect
Down to every font

No matter which way you're written
No matter which way you're drawn
I love that I want you
from dusk till dawn

I don't know how to explain
Why or even how
Even this poem is a bit lame
Down to the way it sounds

The feeling is odd
The emotion gross
So I'm just gonna stop
With one final boast

I want you
Just you
And no one more

"Should I love you?"

When I fall in love, I plumett. I plumett face first from space with my heart on my sleeve. Usually though, there's never anyone on the other side to catch me, so I slam onto the hard concrete of rejection and emotion. There's two ways of handling my situation. One, you can always climb back up and fall again desperately hoping this time you don't become a permanent addition to the sidewalk and someone catches you. Or one could take the route that I've chose. It's a safer route, but it's one you will need to take alone. You stop leaping at the chance of love and affection and become as hard as the concrete you once smashed into. Yet there is one dangerous downfall. If you so happen to choose my hidden path and find yourself falling still, you better hope that there is someone to catch you. Why? Because when jello falls it may bruise but it will bounce back. However, when concrete falls and breaks, the impact is much more devastating. So to the next girl that makes me fall off this ledge, I need to know. Should I love you?

WE'RE NOT CAMPING

I slept outside once, but I've never been camping. I've slept in a tent under the stars and made a fire to keep warm. My family was there with me. They've never been camping. I've been cold and wet. I've been hungry and scared, but I've never been camping. I've sold cans, bottles, plastic, anything I could find. I've survived the freezing cold nights, and I've survived the hungry days. I even manage to survive the questions, but one thing I couldn't get through was the blissfulness of ignorance. A kid in my class said, "I saw you and your family camping." I just replied... "We're not camping."

THROUGH A HAMPS KID'S EYES

We were the only generation of kids at the time. Even in a place like the hamps we made a childhood of what we had. The older we got the more we were able to see. It was like being a kid at a concert who couldn't see the stage or hear the music, because we were too small, so instead of rocking out, we played in our own world. Our world was everything; our capital was 5th Street. The hamps kids never really left 5th Street, and if we did it was like going to some other country. Being stuck in the house was just as bad as a jail sentence to us. We didn't have much in this world of ours, but we had each other. Everyday we were with one another. We took care of each other and even fought like family. All the hamps kids ever needed was 5th Street and the kids who ruled it. However, that didn't last. As we grew taller we got to see a little more of the stage. Our ears got a little close to the speakers and suddenly we could hear the music. The music changed us. It introduced to the real world. It showed us that the monsters that we feared were nothing compared to the ones that didn't hide under the bed. These monsters wore uniforms, suits, badges. These monsters lied. They told us that they were family, that they were teachers and mayors and polices officers who would protect us from the real world. These monsters fed on worlds like 5th Street. The hamps kids never stood a chance. The monsters stole our world, our home. They turned us against each other, killing off the weak. Those who survived found new families. Families that fought other families who lived on the other side town. Those who didn't survive, their minds are being controlled. Whatever they put in their bodies makes them feel happy, makes them escape the music and go back to the way things were. For just ten dollars a dime bag they can go back to the world that was destroyed, ten dollars and a little bit of soul. There was one more group however. They did not die, and they did not just survive. They were the ones who thrived. They were the strongest of them all. Sadly, they will be the next monsters.

YOU BROKE ME.

I was cracked when I met you and you saw inside.
You heard my stories and knew I lied.
You felt the pain I wanted to hide.
You saved a life that wanted to die.
You gained my trust and chipped away the stone.
You came inside and I was no longer alone.
You made me smile until my cheeks were sore.
And when I needed love you gave me yours.
You gave me hope and a reason to fight.
You gave me joy and became my light.
Everyday I loved you more and more.
Now that you're gone my heart's in mourn.
To see you smile and just walk away.
Knowing I could never make you stay.
Wondering if you were ever there.
Doubting the fact that you ever cared.
Sad thing is you're still perfect in my mind
Blaming myself for your crime.
Scared to reach out and grab a new light.
Dying for a reason to continue my fight.
Maybe you were never meant to stay.
But you broke me when you walked away.
I can't blame you I was cracked when we met.
I was too much of a burden... to cracked of a step.

CHILDHOOD DREAMS 1

There was something so pure about what we dreamed of as kids. During this time in our lives we never thought about how much money a job would make us. Most importantly, we never thought what our job title would mean to other people. If we thought it will be cool to be a professional pizza eater than that's what we would do for the rest of our lives. What made this part of our lives so pure and innocent is that we only did what made us happy. Sure as an adult or even in our late teens, we see a mind set such as this to be a bit selfish in a way. Certainly this seems to be a juvenile way of thinking... or is it? Take a moment to think how the world would be if we still thought as kids. Would it be a paradise? Or hell on earth? The reason why we will never be able to get a concrete answer is because as adults we can never ignore the things we have learned about life. To a child this would be a paradise. However, as adults we know that if everyone did what they want we would most certainly run into "wants" that could be from inconvenient to downright horrific. Perhaps a question that we might be better off figuring out an answer to is not what would a world like that would be, but instead when did our "wants" become so corrupt that we could never have them.

TEARS OF A TIGER

Smile baby boy smile.
We all know it's who you are.
Let us see those deep cheeks.
Let it cover your scar.

Don't feel, please don't.
It's not manly to cry.
You're so smart, so brave.
We know you don't want to die.

Shush man shush
You're getting to my nerves
Just take a long drive
Be careful on the curves

Slow down, slow down!
You're going to fast
Don't you see that pole?
You're going to crash!

What's that in your eyes?
Why are you tightening your grip?
Is this what you want?
Are you ready to quit?

Crunch car crunch
Squeal tires squeal
Who's in the car?
Who's behind the wheel?

Drip blood drip
I don't like the taste
It's filling my mouth
And covers my face

Hang on kid, just hang
Have you drank tonight?
Who are you?
Are you alright?

Breath buddy breath
You're going to be okay
You're going to live long and happy
Help is on the way.....

VALUABLE LESSONS

"The most valuable lessons are the ones taught through pain." I remember wondering what my second grade teacher meant when she said that. Even more so, I remember how much she changed that year. She wasn't as nice as she used to be. It was like she was a whole different person. She even changed her last name to match her new personality. When I was thirteen I thought I had an answer. Whenever I did something wrong that lead to pain, I learned what not to do. Every time I fell off my bike I got better. Every time I touched something hot and got burned I became more aware. Then a few years past and now I was fifthteen. Then I thought my second grade teacher was choosing her words wisely and creatively saying... well, saying we needed an ass whooping. I found that funny, because she knew we would never understand what she meant. I thought I had it all figured out until my junior year of high school. You see, I was never going to really understand the lesson because it was a valuable lesson, and as you know, "the most valuable lessons are the ones taught through pain". At this time I had my first heartbreak. There has never been a more fitting word than heartbreak. Everything changed for me after that. My friends changed, my interest changed, I changed. As pain changed me, like touching a hot stove, I became more aware. Now, I remember my teacher's personality change, and most importantly, the change of her last name. As kids we thought she just got married and started to change like people do when they get into a relationship. Unfortunately, I now know better. It wasn't the change of new love but of a love lost. My teacher didn't get married and change her last name as well as her personality, she got divorced. Her "new" name was one she had forgotten, and her "new" personality was a failing attempt to build back what had been broken down. To think nine years after leaving that class she would still be teaching me lessons is amazing. It goes to show how much we evolve over the years. It took seven million years for Australopithecus to become Homo Sapiens and about nine years for a boy to become a man.

SHADOWS

Look Up, look right, look left, look down
You're all alone without a sound
There's a gentle breeze through the trees
That makes the silence bring you to your knees

Alone to see into the deathly stare
Trying to find someone who truly cares
Behind your mask you never grin
Beneath my grasp you cannot win

Look into my eyes and feel our heart
It has beat the same since the start
Doubt yourself and dim your shine
Forever in dark will you be mine

You can't escape your reflection
Even if you change the direction
Even if you lead your life as cattle
You will always be haunted by your shadow

"IDENTITY FRAUD"

In the world of white collar crimes, identity fraud can be one of the worst things to become a victim to. Everything you worked so hard to get can be claimed by someone else in the blink of an eye. Even who you are can easily be swiped away from you. No one is safe from this crime, not even the lower middle class people of Fifth Street. However, there was a different type of identity fraud that I've dealt with. Being mistaken for someone you're not was even more dangerous than someone taking who you are. I had a younger friend name Dawayne. I felt like a big brother to him even though I was only three years older. One day, Dwayne and I were walking home after curfew. It was pitch black outside with a few dim streetlights that only shine directly below them, leaving most of the area around them dark. When we got about half way home we heard rapid footsteps getting closer. Before we could fully turn around, Dawayne was on the ground with a gun held to the back of his head. Now, every movie and made up scenario will have you think your "survival instinct" will suddenly activate and you become some amazing superhero who could disarm him in one move. Unfortunately, that's far from true. The truth is your survival instinct will tell you "if you don't move, you won't get hurt," and you stand there frozen with fear not knowing what to do. Besides, what could I do? What could a fourteen year old boy do to protect his eleven year old friend? The answer is absolutely nothing. As I stood there frozen, the man turned my friend around to look him in the eyes before he killed him. When he saw the terrified look on a kid's face he just shook his head and laughed, "Haha, sorry little man. I thought you were someone else...."

"AMERICAN GIRL"

There is a story of an American girl. She has no name, no home, and no future. However, her past is what she is known by. Pale, thin, with scars behind her eyes that match the ones on her wrist. With her mind weakened by poverty and circumstance, it appeared as if she was an empty shell of girl. This changed starting at fifthteen. Here, it was hardly even noticeable. She went through the motions of a normal teenage girl, from parties to relationships and friends all the same. It appeared that everything was fine, at least everything on the outside. Through the shell of this teenage girl, there was a small crack that slowly leaked out her soul, a crack so small and so absolute it was ignored. Through time and the stress of life, the crack in her shell grew little by little, every day leaking out more and more of the inner filling of feeling and emotion. Slowly, she began to change and felt everything less and less. Break ups and betrayal hurt less and new love felt dim. Now, at sixteen, she began to notice. She tried everything she could to fill the void inside her. She turned to sex, drugs, and alcohol, none of which made her feel the way she wanted for more than just one night at a time. Now seventeen, she can't recall the last few months, jumbled up into a blurry haze of long nights and recovery based mornings. Booze just leave her numb, and drugs leave her vulnerable. Desperate to feel something, she takes the blade from her razor, presses it against her wrist, and begins to cut deeply, too deeply. Blood pours from her arm. She realizes her mistake too late and passes out. The American girl from a small town where none knew her name. Now all know her story. Every seminar and suicide prevention phone line tells her story. They tell those in need to "find their light". The American girl called once before. She only had a single question: What good is a light in an empty room? The operator replied: "So you can see where to put the furniture." I bet she would've loved to hear that answer, but she hung up her lifeline a few moments too early.

AMERICAN GIRL

She listens to her heart
That beats through her chest
She's failed from the start
Despite giving it her best
She's out of hope
And she's out of time
She can't seem to cope
Without a line.
Without a nic
Without a smoke
She cannot fix
What has been broke
Reaching for a hand
Drowning in shame
She can't understand
The thoughts in her brain
They flow through her mind
They stain her soul
They break the binds
So she can't go home
American girl
Where none knew her name
Will never be forgotten
Through the memories of pain.

MY CREATIVE WORLD

I never lost my imagination growing up. For the most part, it could be a good thing. I used to dream of entire worlds where I was a hero like in the video games I'd play, boldly charging at danger with my sword in my hand. I fantasized about being my favorite mutant hunting vampires and ghouls, even having the same hair style. Normally when people get older they stop daydreaming about being the hero in a dark world. As for me, when I got older, I just fantasized about whatever I was into at the time. Then, I was a monster-slaying mutant, and now, I'm a demon hunter riding in an old-school car with my brother. I wanted to be my heroes so bad that I was okay with being in their world full of monsters and evil. As of now, however, that's starting to change. I still spend way too much time daydreaming, but the nature of which is more peaceful. My most recent daydream was a friend and I that I never saw as a romantic interest now being my wife. We're sitting in a brick kitchen with a wooden table and chairs drinking coffee out of white porcelain cups. We're not saying anything, but on occasion we would look up, lock eyes, laugh a little, and go back to drinking. Every time I see her look up at me, the sun is shining behind her, and it looks as if she's glowing, despite the fact that the only window is to her side. But in my creative world, the laws of physics or love do not apply. The strangest thing about it isn't the romantic interest or the sun breaking common sense or even the fact that in real life I don't drink coffee. The strangest thing about it is that I'm not a hero in a broken world, but just someone who truly feels loved. I find myself having these daydreams more often than not, daydreams in my creative world where I'm happy and it's sunny and noisy and full of smiles. When I used to daydream about being some sort of hero, I left the dream feeling as if I just watched my favorite tv show, and I was the guest star. Now, when I leave my cheerful daydreams I look up from my cup to see no one there, no one smiling or laughing and the sun dimly shining through the curtain covered window. I feel like I'm back in that tv show I loved so much, full of monsters and darkness, only this time I'm not the hero. I'm not even the villain. I'm just a guy in an empty room sipping juice from a coffee cup and waiting for the credits to roll.

"DERANGED THOUGHTS"

It's really complicated and really fucked up, but I feel emotionless towards everything happening around me. Things that I should be overwhelmingly concerned about and I'm feeling nothing. Then there's this other thing that changes that, that makes me feel like it is perfect in every flaw and perk and that nothing can ever be wrong with it. But I had this feeling before, and I ended up in a really, really, really fucked up spot, and I couldn't handle it happening again. But you still hope that' it's different because, the thing is different even though you feel the same. But let's say you get past that and are ready to take the risk again. There's another risk. Let's say you can spend your life with this thing, but you can only do it at a painful distance. However, if you reach out for it one of two things will happen. One, you grab on tight and you're never forced to let go and you never want to. Or, when you reach out, it slips away from your fingertips, and it's gone. You're not even able to enjoy from a distance.

DAILY THOUGHTS

Dying for a reason to live.
Stealing something to give.
Hurting for a way to feel.
Faking to see what's real.
Lying to hide the truth.
Going down to reach the roof.

My actions are wrong but they're my actions alone.
Good deeds are forgotten while mistakes are stoned.
Scars try to hide while fake smiles are shown.
Surrounded by people and being alone.

Misunderstood and unexplained.
Ending love turns to endless pain.
Abandoning. Forgetting. Eventually moving on.
The bonds are broken, buried now gone.

Memories bring pain,
crying brings shame.
No way to explain
Why I still feel the same.

Alone with the voices that make life harder.
Keeping quiet to not be a bother.
Scared to turn and beg for help.
No way to explain how I felt.

No honor in taking the life I call my own
Regardless of love we all die alone.
Regardless of hate we are all the same.
1 nose, 2 feet, 1 heart, 1 brain.

Now you know all my faults
I'm more psychotic than you ever thought.
Deranged, ill, and a lack of social skill
Crazy is the word to describe what's real.

"POETRY IN THE DARK"

poetry in the dark, where people can't read your pain
the words look different but they feel the same
wearing a mask to hide who you are
wearing long sleeves to hides your scars

cover your shame, hide your fears
crack a smile, wipe your tears
tell them jokes,make them laugh
don't let them see your path

cover your tracks, cover them well
it's hard to explain your life of hell
they can never know, they never should
poetry in the dark is never understood

"CRUMBLING CRUMBS"

the walls are falling, the floors are gone
the sky is dark, the nights are long
she said goodbye, she says she's done
my heart is heavy, my body is numb

she was my world, my light in the night
she knows my past, she knows my fight
she felt my pain, she heard my cry
but she's gone now, I don't know why

she's in my thoughts, she's in my mind
this is my punishment, my word my crime
to lose what you love, a fate worst than death
my world is gone, I have nothing left

I beg not to leave, I can't force your stay
stay with me please, don't walk away
you're my world, you're all i need
it's only goodbye if you let it be

"FLOWER PETALS"

flower petals floating in the wind
there's no worry, no pain, no sin
we believe we are free, but that's not what we see
what we see is ourselves and what were to be

Truth is they are now alone
blown from their family, stolen from their home
these petals we see are far from free
these petals are slaves to their destiny

to have no control of our hearts, mind, or soul
how can we call our actions our own
the moment we're free is when we're enslaved
from the time we are born, our deaths have been made

What's the point of going if there's only one road
how can we rebel if there is no throne
our choices are made, our days are numbered
the reward for survival is eternal slumber

but there's a bright side to an end so grim
a small ray of sunshine on days so dim
for the hate we take there's love to give
because death awaits is our reason to live

"SCARS"

tell me a story with no words
show me your scars, scratches, and burns
let me see your pain, show me your heart
be my sunshine when my world gets dark

bleed my blood and feel my shame
be there for me and I'll do the same
stand still when my monsters release
hold me tight until they retreat

you became my world, my love, my life
I grabbed at my chest and pulled out your knife
I felt the pain only in my heart
and once again my world was dark

it hurts to see you but I can't look away
the pain won't leave because you won't stay
I didn't think you cared or if you should
I can't believe you did what I never could

"CONVERSATIONS WITH DEATH"

I'm looking for a replacement
to fill the void in my soul
to ease the aching in my heart
and change the story that I hold

I'm looking for a healer
of divine powers and skills
to do away with my scars
at the cost of my tears

I'm looking for an answer
to who I am
to why hang on
to a lifeless stem

I'm looking for a life
where I'm looking no more
where the answers are clear
where I'm free to soar

I'm looking for a death
that I can call my own
that I can close my eyes
and lay still as stone

I'm asking this of you
the one they call death
to end my search
and grant my request

"CONVERSATIONS WITH MAN"

Yes it is true.
Death is my name.
But your request.
Is one in the same.

I've roamed this world.
Taking lives and souls.
Of empty vessels.
With stories untold.

Lives lost in secret.
Bodies never to be found.
Lives taken away.
Without ever a sound.

No voice for the dead.
Their stories won't be told.
They're mine for the keeping.
And none have I sold.

Be happy with your story.
It's the only one you get.
Because when your soul comes to me.
Your life will be spent.

YOU….AGAIN

I wanted to write something original
I wanted to write something new
I wanted to write anything just anything
Okay fine I wanted to write about you
I wanted to write about your eyes
I wanted to write about your lips
I wanted to write about your sexy perfect hips.
I wanted to write about my dreams
Which all included you
I wanted to write about how much I
Wanted them to become true
I wanted to write the stories that I'd hope to tell our kids
I wanted to show the world to you
So that I can call dibbs.
But most of all I wanted you
Whether it was day or night
Mostly I wanted you
But I fear the time is not right
So all I can do is want
And dream the time away
And hope that my want grows
And pulls you toward my way.

"A STUDENTS HOMAGE"

How often do you get to change someone's life? Whether or not they know it, teachers change lives every day. A good teacher can get you through the school year and even help you stay on the path to graduation. I have teachers who have done that for me, and they deserve the utmost respect. However, this homage is for the special few who absolutely changed my life, who did above and beyond, not because they were on the clock, but because they really cared. Everything you six have done for me will never be forgotten. I owe this to you.

MR. GAGE

Mr. Gage, I was one of your fallen soldiers in your war on gammer. I spent very little time in your english class my sophomore year, but that didn't stop your faith in me. What you gave me is something most people never get. You gave me a chance my senior year. I spent my whole school career slacking, because I planned to just join the military until I died or retired, because I felt there was nothing else I could do. I felt that I didn't have any talent, any motivation, or anything at all to offer the world. You were the first teacher to make me feel otherwise. Although it took me until my senior year to take you up on your offer, you allowed me to act in one of your drama plays. You brought out a talent I never even knew I had. After the first play, you gave me a lead role in the next. You may have just saw it as another kid in another play, but to me.... to me you gave me purpose. I was no longer just a kid. I was James, the nerdy kid who got his first girlfriend, or I was a teenager whose parents never let him live his life the way he wanted to. You opened up a whole new world to me. You gave me a dream to chase and a goal to reach. I will never forget that.

MR. DAILEY

Mr. dailey, in today's world every celebrity has a scandal waiting to be overturned. You gave me something that no youth has anymore. You provided me a positive male role model. Every day that it was raining or too cold, I knew that when I walked down the hallway to my homeroom, you were there with a smile and your giant hands high fiving every student that walked pass. What made you special was that your attitude wasn't you ignoring the problems of life, but you accepting them for what they were and not letting them control who are. If there was any problem any student had they could come to you for a real answer. You didn't diminish our problems by saying, "ahh just smile through it." No, not you Mr.Dailey. Your answers acknowledged our problems as real problems and not just teenagers complaining about minor issues. You gave consoling and wisdom even though you were closer to our age than any other teacher. I hope one day I could be half as great as the man I know you to be.

MRS. WILSON

Mrs. Wilson, words can't describe how much you've helped your students. When times were dark and we were at our lowest, you were there. You've saved so many kids with suicidal thoughts and unplanned pregnancy's, to divorces and crippling break-ups, all while battling every injury you had in the past years. You've had more surgeries than most people can count, yet you refuse to give up. Your talks on suicide and depression helped me understand what was going on in my head. Although I never said it to you outloud, you knew who I was through my writing. I knew every time you asked how I was doing it was because you cared. I said I was fine and gave you a hug, but you knew the truth. After my "accident" you were the person I came closest to telling what happened. I don't why I never told you. Honestly, I didn't think I needed to. Regardless of how I was doing, I knew you were always there. I think that's all I needed. You gave me a piece of your heart so that mine could keep pumping. For someone like you, I can't find good enough words to give thanks, so instead I guess all I can say is thank you.

MRS. BENNETT

A usual teacher's work is done during the summer. The average teacher loses contact with a student after they graduate. Mrs. Bennett, you are far from usual and way above average. I will never forget our inside jokes where we would burst into laughter in the middle of the class. Although that definitely sets you aside from any other teacher, that's not why I wish to give you thanks. In the middle of the summer after I graduated, I sent you an email late at night, because I felt like a loser. I saw everyone getting ready for college and moving on with their lives, and all I had to offer was a full time job I was miserable at and high school memories to reminisce about. I felt that at my old age of eighteen I should be starting a career and a family and already be successful in life. Now, any teacher could have ignored that email or even waited until the morning to reply. Instead, you wrote back almost instantly, telling me that I was crazy to feel that way and I have years to decide what to do. That was exactly what I needed to hear. In my time of need, you gave me a friend. You talked to me about my potential and what I could achieve, until I had new faith in myself. Mrs. Bennett, you are truly one of a kind.

MS. PERRELLA

Ms. Perrella, I know you will never forget that fifth period english my senior year, some for good reason. You pushed so hard and didn't budge when we pushed back. I never thought someone so small could be so strong. I'm glad you pushed everyone so hard. Who knows where I'd be if you never taught me what a vignette was. You helped me expand on my writing more than any other english teacher I had. You allowed me to express creativity more than ever before. Creativity is illegal in most schools, but you had no issue breaking that law for us. Speaking in front of the class and listening to others present their writings showed many of us that we are far from alone in the problems we face. You united a class with more social groups than books. When we shared our work, we felt equal. That year, you gave all of us unity.

MR. BRUNO

Mr. Bruno, there is no secret that you were like a father to me. I never understood why you took an interest in me, but I'm so glad that you did. You inspired me to become more than what I thought my self-worth was. Your struggle from a 1.5 gpa and a 13 A.C.T score to now teaching law and psychology is nothing short of amazing. You taught me more outside of class than any classroom I've been in. Most of all, when everyone was against your decision to put me on your mock trial team, you stood your ground that year, and we were the first team in our school's history to make it to state. Even after I graduated, you never stopped being there for me. Mr. Bruno, you are my true hero. You may not be the tallest or youngest or even the smartest, but you are one hell of a guy. Your most valuable gift to me was inspiration.

"THE DELIVERY BOY"

Where I lived growing up, delivery was never an option. It's a rude awaking when you hear it for the first time. Imanage this, you order pizza or chinese food from your favorite place. You have your money and a tip in cash ready to go. You place your order just the way you like it, and the employee on the phone asks for your address. Without a second thought, you give the employee your address, and the line goes quiet for a moment. When they return, they politely inform you that "delivery services are currently unavailable in your area." Now, in case you were wondering, that may be what they say, but that's not what we hear. Translation: sorry, but we don't have a delivery boy who hates his life so much that he would risk it going to a neighborhood as bad as yours.

Come to think about it, I have a story about a delivery boy. Now he never worked for any pizza shop or anything like that. In fact, he didn't even have a ride to make his "deliveries," but he always got to his stops on time. I remember he ran everywhere with a brown book bag, and when i saw him again, this time coming from the other direction, the book bag was black and a lot smaller. I never ordered anything from him, but I do know a junkie that stayed in the abandoned house next to my grandmother's. You see, the story goes that this particular junkie wasn't always a junkie. However, he broke a golden rule, something to do with using his on supply. One day, the junkie didn't have have his book bag to give to the delivery boy, and without his black backpack, he could never get the brown book bag, which was a problem for the junkie. Junkies are not known for their reasonable behavior, so when the delivery boy arrived on time like always, the junkie had a "reasonable" offer for the boy. The offer was to give him the book bag now and next time, he would have two book bags for the boy. When the delivery boy immediately declined the offer and demanded the black bag, the junkie then offered, "give me the brown bag now and next time i will have three bags for you, even more then normal." The delivery boy thought and thought, but eventually declined the offer, so the junkie came up with his most reasonable offer he thought of all day. He would just take the bag and give the delivery boy nothing but a stab womb to the neck. Apparently, it worked at out first, until that abandoned house was burned down with the sleeping junkie in it. At the time, I never knew the lesson of that story. The only thing I could think about was that's probably why the pizza man never comes around.

"I WANT TO BE FREE"

I want to be free
free from the shackles of poverty
no more shame for me
if only I were free

I want to be free
free enough to stand tall
attend elegant masquerades
even the queen's ball

I want to be free
free from the pain of hunger
free from the cold
free to one day growing old

I need to be free
free enough to fly
free enough to live
free enough to die

I want to be free

"I'M OKAY"

You know what the worst part about growing up hungry was? You constantly had to pretend you weren't hungry. I mean, kids were already making fun of your old clothes and nameless brand shoes and how skinny you were. The last thing you needed to do is give the class comedians more material to work with. How would that comeback even work? "Hey twiggy why you so skinny?" "Because my mom can't afford to feed me, and my sister's by herself while also keeping our hotel room paid for a few more days…..fatso." Yeah, no thanks. So I always pretended not to be hungry, even if that meant passing up meals. Anything to make them believe I wasn't starving. I even believed it myself, until the growls of my empty stomach snapped me out of it. However, any time that I was offered free food or a donation from teachers and "concerned parents" I would just say, "No…. I'm okay."

"The hotel room"

I didn't understand that living in a hotel room was bad. How could an elementary kid even put that as a bad thing? We went from sleeping on my dad's friend's floor to our very own hotel room. It didn't hit me until I was in school. It was a normal day, until my teacher called me up to the class. We had to describe what we saw in our house using nouns, verbs, and adjectives and pointing out what words were what. So, I started by saying proudly, "I don't live in a house. My family stays in a hotel room." The class bursted into laughter as if I was the greatest class clown to have ever lived. Their faces were bright red and mouths so wide open I could almost see the food from their full bellies. They laughed right out of there name brand shoes. Maybe they were laughing at me or they thought I was joking. My teacher said I didn't have to share, and we moved on from the topic in general. I thought about it all day until I went home. I asked my brother why it was so funny. He just said I'll understand when I get older.

SCARED TO SMILE

My life is turning around.
Screaming turned into subtle sounds.
Whispers are still love bound.
But the love is different now.

She makes me forget the pain I felt.
I've started to enjoy the hand I've dealt.
My heart and soul have begun to melt.
Because she will leave if I asked for help.

She doesn't know what I've done.
She doesn't know what I've become.
She doesn't know what makes me numb.
If she knows then she won't be the one.

I can't hide this truth forever.
Stuck in this stormy weather.
Hoping I truly get better.
Broken, shattered, and taped together.

"NEW SHOES"

I used to love getting new shoes. I always thought that when I got new shoes I could run faster than my old ones. Every time, I got faster and faster, I ran harder and longer, faster and faster. I started to think I was just as fast as every other kid with name brand shoes on. The newer the shoes, the faster I was. The faster I was, the closer to the other kids I got. It was like I could run so fast that I would break out of poverty and be with the other kids. My name brand shoes made me feel like I was one of them. The rest of the year it felt like everyone forgot I was poor. I was a kid with name brand shoes now, and nothing could catch me: not being poor, not being hungry, not even being homeless. With these new shoes i could run away from it all. The only problem about new shoes is that they don't stay new forever. Coming back to school the next year with the same shoes put me right back where I started. I guess poverty got some new shoes too.

I HAVE TO LET GO

One of my biggest fears is getting used to someone. The thought of someone being there every day and night for me excites me. In fact, that was one of the greatest parts about being in love for me. To think day in and day out there was someone, anyone who was genuinely interested in me. All good things, however, must come to an end, and for me the absence was what drove me crazy. How could someone go from talking to a person every day and night, to never again? By all means, I understand a gradual drift apart over time, but the sudden stops were painful. Any shrink could easily say I feel this way, because I have abandonment issues starting from my childhood. I think that's crap. Regardless of some traumatic event in one's childhood, no one likes being alone.

"JUST LEAVE"

You do know I'm crazy.
Don't you know I'm insane?
They say my head is chaos.
With very little brain.
Dark, twisted, and really corrupt
Look at me girl, can't you tell I'm nuts!?
Haha girl I have issues from here to the moon
I should be tied up and thrown in a padded room
Run while you can, get the hell away
I have issues with people that stay
You're just going to leave, LIKE EVERYONE ELSE.
GOD DAMNIT I'M CRAZY, I REALLY NEED HELP.
Do you think I feel like you? Do you think I care?
I feel empty inside, because there's nothing there.
I'm dark baby, rotten to core.
Just leave like everyone else, I'll just add one more.
One more to the heartache, one more song
One more thing that I just get wrong.
So go ahead and leave, it doesn't even hurt
I'll just be fixing myself, I could use some work

"BLANK FACES"

There were those on Fifth Street that we called blank faces. Blank faces were scarier than any Halloween mask you could find. Every event, no matter how happy or sad, there was absolutely no emotion in their eyes. Hearing one of them speak was unsettling. It was like they had absolutely no feelings towards anything. Blank faces, we called them. We were taught to show them respect them. We never knew why blank faces were so important. Apparently cops hated them. My brother would say talking to the blank faces was like talking to a brick wall; no matter how much you threaten them or how much time they're facing, they will just sit there staring at you with a blank face.

"LOUD SILENCE"

is anyone there?
is anyone there?
to help me through
my thoughts of despair?

can anyone hear?
can anyone hear?
the loud silence
that floats through the air?

can anyone see?
can anyone see?
those soulless blank faces
surrounding me?

can anyone feel?
can anyone feel?
the hunger pains of a child
dreaming of the next meal?

I can hear
I can see
through the echos of silence
through the sound of quite

I can feel
I am there
to speak for the voiceless
and tend to their care

Am I alone
to tend on my own
or will you speak
for those to weak

I guess we'll see
I guess we'll see
if you succumb to fate
or chase destiny

JUST ME

My parents divorce was understandably hard on everyone. That being said, everyone broke into groups. My mother quickly got remarried to a guy she hardly knew. None of us went to the wedding, and a lot of change came with it. My mother turned into a religious, mindless robot who followed orders from her new master she called husband. It often felt that we were second place to her when he was in the picture. Although she didn't treat us right, when it came to bills and school, she was our support. My mother has done some bad things in her past, some I hope she regrets, but in order to make mistakes you have to be trying. My father, on the other hand, wasn't around at all. I would remember calling him every weekend asking if he was coming to pick me up. I remember him saying he would be there a 6:30. I would get so excited and pack everything I wanted to show him. My mom would tell me he wasn't going to show up, but I had faith in my dad. I would even sit outside and wait for him, jumping up anytime a car would ride pass. It was never him. 6:30 came and went and still no dad. 7:30 past, 8:30 past, and around 9pm I would go in the house. All my siblings knew he wasn't coming, but I guess I had to learn for myself. What made it worse, every weekend would go the same. He would say he's on his way and for a few hours a little boy full of hope would sit and wait for his father to keep his promise. It never happened.

LATE NIGHTS

On late nights where I can't sleep.
I think about promises I couldn't keep.
I think about days where I couldn't feel.
But showed a smile that I knew wasn't real.

I think about my mother and the things she'll say.
I think about my father who refused to stay.
I beat myself down as if they haven't enough.
I think about the times that were unbearably rough.

On nights where I can't sleep
I cover my head in my sheets.
I lay still and let time flee.
And wonder what makes me.
Was it being homeless and poor.
Was it selling from door to door.
Is it my mental state of mind.
That bounces from evil to kind.

Late nights are all the same.
I leave my thoughts untamed.
My feelings run wild and bite.
My actions are one star in a late night.

APOLOGIES

Kids can be cruel. I myself, unfortunately, have been on both sides of bullying. With my past experience, you would think I would be the last kid to become a bully. Sadly, that's untrue. Now making fun of your friends is one thing. It's different, because when they really need you you're there for them. This isn't the case when it comes to Josh. I picked on him, because I thought he was weak. Or maybe I was just jealous. He was small, skinny, and pale. He wasn't the fastest or the coolest or anything I tried to be. He didn't care about what made him cool or uncool, and everyone made fun of him. Despite all of that, when he wasn't being tormented, Josh was the happiest kid I knew. Everyday he came to school with a smile. He didn't have new clothes to show off or a cool new haircut, yet, he didn't care. He didn't care what he didn't have, because he loved what he had. Deep down at the time, I hated him for that. He was happy without everything I thought would make me happy. I thought of Josh as weak, small, and unimportant. I couldn't have been more wrong. Josh, to put up with my crap and everyone else's all through middle school shows how strong you really are. The very fact that I still think about how much of a loser I was to pick on you shows how significant you were in my life. I want to apologize to you in person one day. I don't feel like a crappy message on social media is enough, and if I could

I would do it on national TV, but as of right now, this is best I can do. I'm sorry for the way I treated you in middle school. I'm sorry for the way everyone treated you. One of these days I'm going to make it up to you.

"FUNNY PAIN"

let them talk, let them laugh
make them burn, hope they crash
kill their hopes, smash their dreams
take off your mask to make them scream

bleed your hate scream your rage
flip the script then rip the page
show them the monster you truly are
stand to be praised, force their awe

they laugh out loud while you grin in the dark
filled with rage in hope of a spark
explode on the canvas, release through your pen
make them fear your passion, not your sin

let them hate, let them judge
make them push but never budge
stand PROUD, stand STRONG
Hear their lies and prove them wrong

Just me... Again

While my mother had her head in the clouds and my father was God knows where, my sisters were the closest things to me. For the most part, that's not saying much. My oldest sister was out on her own already, but the three that lived with me were teenage girls going through puberty and a divorce. I understand that they were going through a mess. Most of the time they stayed in their room and talked to each other. For whatever it was they had the three of them. For a while, they did just fine with just the three of them. My brother was gone like my dad. He lived with us but was hardly ever home. What can you expect from a sixteen year boy with his own car? He wouldn't be caught dead in the house. It seemed everyone had what they wanted, almost everyone.

FALL

while the leaves change so do I
the leaves may fall
but the trees never cry

For they know it will return
when the soil is rich
and the air is warm

shall I change as well
shed my skin
to escape my hell

to be born once more
when I am rich
with an open door

no tears will be dropped
when I trade my skin
for one at the top

walking around
in one last skin
ever so proud

"MAYBE NOT"

Self doubt is a lingering stench on my soul. Every dream I've had has always been thought with the phrase "maybe not". When I ran track, I thought, MAYBE I CAN GET FIRST TODAY, quickly followed by a maybe not. Even when it came to mock trail, I thought, MAYBE WE CAN MAKE IT TO STATE! Then creeping up the side of my thoughts, a quiet maybe not. Should I try out for drama club? Maybe not. Will Oprah ever read my book? Maybe not. Well that voice is still there in the back of my mind, but this time I have something to say to it. I tried out for drama club, and I got a part. I placed first in my 4 by 4 relay in track, and my mock trial team made it to state that year. I may not be a famous actor and Oprah might not ever read this book. Maybe I should just give up... maybe not.

"JUST ME... ONE LAST TIME"

Everyone had their own outlet for handling a broken home. My brother, dad, and eldest sister took to the outside world. My mother took to her new husband, and my three sisters who lived at home took to each other. So where does that leave a young boy that has no idea what's going on? It leaves him alone. For the first time in his life, he felt alone. From having a house with five other siblings and both parents, to not even seeing half his family on a monthly basis, this became the biggest turning point in his life. He always felt as if he was in the way. For the most part, he didn't even consider himself a part of the family. Even being called somewhere, it was always Glorese, Gloria, Monica AND Malcom. Why did he have to be "And" Malcom, as if they all wanted to be detached from him? Maybe it was just a side effect of being the youngest, but with a house full of strangers who wanted nothing to with a lonely boy, it felt like much more. With no one to turn to, his best friend was his thoughts. Still, juvenile and untamed, he had no idea how to talk to them, only to listen. His thoughts weren't always the best company. However, it was the only company he had. Although he was only able to listen at the time, his thoughts only focused on him, just him. He was no longer "And Malcom." He was no longer alone. He was me... just me.

"Loud lullaby"

Can you tell the difference between fireworks and gunshots? It's easy. Fireworks are what you hear when it's the Fourth of July or some other celebration, and gunshots are what you hear when you go to bed at night. What? You don't hear gunshots at night? Sure you do. You just don't know it. It's the loud BOOM before you hear the police sirens. What? You don't hear police sirens at night? Sure you do. It makes the same sound as the ones that come to your house when your parents are fighting. The police don't come to your house? Your parents don't fight? Wait, where do you live again? Ohh.... Where do I live? The hamps... Yeah. Yeah. I know, your mom said you can't go there.

"TO BE A SOLDIER"

grab your gun grab your chute
fall from above and prepare to shoot
win the battle survive the war
avenge your fallen no time to mourn

reload your bag pop that smoke
put on your mask and don't you choke
this is not our war but this is our fight
we killed today and we're killing tonight

sleep tight but never dream
don't let your brothers hear you scream
stay on watch stay alert
don't let your enemies know you're hurt

gather your strength embrace your power
more will be here by the hour
fight for freedom fight for glory
come back home to tell the story

"IT'S JUST YOUR PATH"

I never hold any grudges for people who choose to no longer be in my life. If anything I encourage them to follow their path. I have many friends who wouldn't know if I dropped dead. Really though, it's okay. I always felt like I was in the way, so for those people who go where I'm not needed, I embrace them. Fathers, brothers, childhood friends are all the same. There is truly no blame in leaving someone to follow where you want to go. That's what I tell myself at least. So to all my friends who are gone now, there is no hard feeling brother. It's just your path.

A.C.T

I hated the A.C.T. I hated it, because I understood exactly why it was there. It's so much easier to to group people in numbers. The only thing that backs up the A.C.T is just more statistics and tests showing why a different test should be considered when showing how valuable someone else is. This was a legal way for colleges to say, "YOU ARE NOT GOOD ENOUGH FOR US." The education system of America has sucked out creativity and art for a test number. They traded humanity, because it's more convenient to judge someone based off of how smart they are. The reason why creativity is illegal in school is because they can't number the mind. Everything else you do in school can be judged by a number. Do good? 100%! Do bad? 0%! Its nice and easy for people to read a number to determine your worth, your value, your cost. However, what's the price of your mind? What's the price of your story? What's the price of your expression? How much does feeling cost? How much is pride? How much is honnor? How much is faith? It's easy to price the things that keeps the world spinning like gas and food, but the things that make the world stop... they're priceless. Love is priceless. Art is priceless to its creator. Faith is priceless to the believer. Your school will never care what you have inside your heart, because they're to busy trying to put a price tag on your brain.

"STARTING OVER"

I always hated starting over, but it's something we had to do a lot of growing up. Dad lost his job? Start over! Parents are divorced? Start over. Someone break your heart? Start over! My fifth grade year alone I went to three different schools. The problem about starting over is not only getting rid of the good things, but trying to recapture them with something new. We as people rush to get back where we once were without even realizing it will be the very thing to make us start over again. In school, I would try to replace my old friends. In love, I would try to mimic my old memories. Truth is, no one likes starting over. Not because we feel like we have nothing now, but because we feel like we will never get it back. In the back of our minds, things will never be as good.

CAN YOU HEAR ME?

Can hear my cries behind my laughs?
Can you smell my soul after my baths?
Can you hear my heart when it's off beat?
Can you read my words when they're off the sheet?
Can you feel my rhyme when the rhythm is off?
Can you see the butterfly inside every moth?
Can you feel the pain I hold inside?
Can you still feel love if the love has died?
Can you walk away when I'm at your feet?
Can you still win when you feel that you're beat?
Can you see me cry when my eyes are dry?
Can you judge my life when all you see is a lie?
Can you say you will love me forever
and still walk away?
Can you die inside and live another day?

"ABOVE NATURE"

When leaves die in the fall no one thinks anything of it. Everyone just says it's nature and that the leaves will just come back next year. The difference between us and the leaves is that we don't believe we're a part of nature. We believe that we are above it, that we are special. Although, in some ways we are special, we are still not above nature. People don't understand that. That's why we fear death.

We're part of nature just like every living thing here from the grass to the trees. There's no heaven or hell for them. The same goes for us. You're not the first to be afraid of the unknown. People make stories of afterlife to give them false hope of being immortal. Funny thing is, they give their only lives to defend it. What makes life worth living is impacting someone else's life with yours. That's the only heaven or hell we can hope for, to be immortalized in memory or nightmares.

"TRULY IMMORTALIZED"

Let's say this is your life (A).

Now during your lifetime you change the life of (B).

Now you die. However, you live on in the memory of life (B).

Now with your memory, life (B) changes the life of (C).

Life (B) dies but lives on in the memory of life (C). Now, although you died and life (C) has no idea who you are, he\she knows and lives on what you stand for and what you thought (B) your life created an everlasting domino effect, and even though the domino that fell first is now forgotten, everything is different because of that domino, and that first, second, and every domino involved will be immortalized in the effect it made. So for me, heaven is the good memory of you, being immortalized in happiness of a memory. Hell is the same, but in a nightmare. You may die, and your name may be forgotten, but if you make an impact and if you start the fall to your own domino effect, then you will be truly immortalized

"WHAT WILL BECOME OF ME"?

what will become of me
at the end of my time
when death finally comes
to collect his fine

What will happen to my soul
as my body lays to rest
when it becomes too old

will I be remembered for years on end
or be forgotten

will you remember me?

"WHAT TYPE OF MAN WILL I BE TODAY"?

I take the way I appear in public very cautiously. I feel like when people see me, I don't just represent myself or my family, but my entire race, which often brings the question, "What type of man will i be today?" The way society sees the average black man isn't something I wish to be. For the most part, it's like we're just gestures for the "superior race." Every party I went to I was expected to dance or know the latest rap song and have a book bag full of drugs. Sure, I like to dance, and I love rap, and by no means am I a stranger to drugs, but I hated being typed cast. They saw me as black, not Malcom, so I love being able to give the middle finger to everyone who stereotypes me based on my skin. Instead of being a rapper, I became a poet. Instead of coming to school high, I came enlightened and clean. When every other black kid wore sports shoes and baggy jean, I dressed in suits and dress shoes. I did this not only because I liked the way I was, but to be the exception to anything people thought they knew about black people. There was only one setback, however. While I was flipping off the social standard, my very own people looked at me differently. They didn't see that they were being laughed at and not with. They did not see the problem with people acting and talking "Black". My very own people tended to be disgusted by me, because they believed I was trying to be something I wasn't. They believed by dressing different and speaking properly that I was ashamed of who I was. What they didn't realize was that thinking they couldn't be this way was exactly what I was fighting for. They didn't realize that they had the option to be whoever they wanted to be and not just who we were told we were. They didn't realize that they were no longer slaves who had to take orders. It's time for us to choose our own path and to be able to express any form of creativity or art we desire. Understand, you are your own person.We are no longer slaves.

"THE PRICE OF MY LIFE"

What do I cost to the world
what am I worth
about 8.10 an hour
says my manger

what do I cost to the world
what am I worth
that depends on your test score
says college

what do I cost to the world
what am i worth
about 18 years of my life
says my mother

what do I cost to the world
what am I worth
that's up to you to decide
says my teachers

What do I cost to the world
what am I worth
nothing
says my reflection

"THE WITCHES PATH"

Back on Fifth Street, there was a path called "the witches path". Now legend tells it that a witch lived in an old hut in the middle of the path. There was always an old spanish lady telling all the kids to stray far away from this path and to never go there. So as all kids do, we didn't believe her and went to go see it anyway. Boldly going where no kid had gone before, we were armed with sticks and our imagination. We were determined to find this witch. The closer we got, we all expressed what we would do if we found her. There was a large hill in our path. When we got to the top we were able to spot the hut. However, there was something we didn't expect to see. We saw smoke coming from the roof of the hut. Not the type that would suggest a fire, but heat. We never expected to find someone or something living there. We stood there frozen in confusion. We walked slower and slower the closer we got we. Now we are a few feet away from the front door. Suddenly, we heard: BOOM! BOOM! BOOM! Everyone turned and ran for their lives. We stormed up the hill and never looked back. When we asked about the witch to the old spanish lady, she laughed and said: "Were you all expecting a real witch? Sorry baby, those only exist in fairy tales. We just call women that we don't like witches. She shot at me too once, but she's harmless. She never hit anyone other than her late husband. Come to think about it, I think that's how she got the name."

I NEED A DAY

I need a day where the earth just stops. I just need 24 hours where no one is counting. No one is thinking about work the next day or the work they just got done doing. I just need a day where nothing happens. No one is thinking about who they are. No one is thinking about who they love or hate. No one is thinking about their diet or their weight. I need 24 hours where the weight of each and every individual's world, mother, father, and child just falls off their shoulders and everyone floats a little. I just need a day where all the right choices can be made for everyone.

I need a day where I'm not sad or happy or busy. I need a day where I can cry without questioning my manhood. I need a day where I can be weak and fall to my knees and let it out. And when this 24 hours is up the whole world goes as if nothing happened. The tears dry and the screams are silenced. And when every father, mother, brother, sister, or single child picks up the weight of their world and puts it back on their shoulders, we only notice that we sink a little less into the ground. I just need a day.

"KILL ME"

what doesn't kill you leave you broken
the lies that hurt are never spoken
the actions shown are never my own
surrounded by friends and being alone

seeing the pain through a blind man's eyes
hearing the screams of a mute man's cries
thinking the thoughts of a child gone mad
trying to feel a love gone bad

kill me while i'm sleep and subtle
i'll take my life to save you the trouble
a broken heart will remain shattered
when treated like it doesn't matter

"A WORLD WITHOUT ME"

I wonder what it will be
must be a sight to see
how life will go on
in a world without me

How will it change?
Could it be the same?
I wonder what it will be
in a world without me

What impact have i made
that will make the world fade
who will be able to see
the world without me

But i think it would be fine
if the world started anew
But only if it fades me out
to add more of you

About the Author

Born in a family of six, I was the youngest of them. As a child, I always heard about the great things that happened before I was born. However, that's when the good times ended. I didn't feel responsible for the most part, but the coincidence was a bit too much to ignore. Now that my family has families of their own, as the youngest, I'm trying to adjust to a world where I am no longer just one of the kids but my own person.

Printed in the United States
By Bookmasters